SPECIAL TIMES

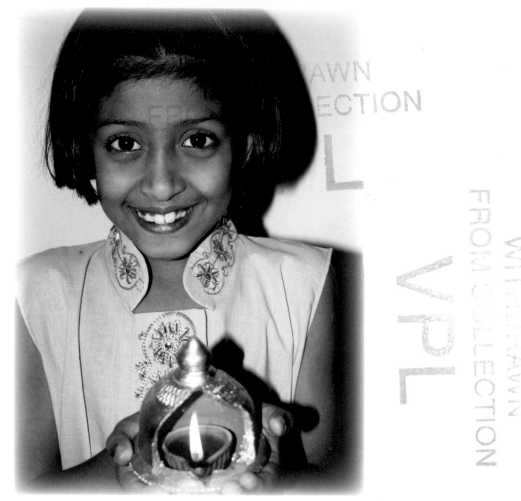

A journey through life in

Hinduism

Jane A. C. West

Consultants: Jay and Seeta Lakhani

Contents

Published by A & C Black
Publishers Limited
36 Soho Square
London W1D 3QY
www.acblack.com

ISBN 978-1-4081-2963-0

Series concept: Suma Din
Series consultant: Lynne Broadbent
Hinduism consultants: Jay and Seeta
Lakhani of the Hindu Academy

Created by Bookwork Ltd, Stroud, UK

A CIP catalogue record for this book is
available from the British Library.

A & C Black uses paper produced with
elemental chlorine-free pulp, harvested
from managed sustainable forests. It
is natural, renewable and recyclable.
The logging and manufacturing process
conform to the environmental regulations
of the country of origin.

Printed in China by Leo Paper Products

All the internet addresses given in this
book were correct at the time of going to
press. The author and publishers regret
any inconvenience caused if addresses
have changed or sites have ceased to
exist, but can accept no responsibility for
any such changes.

10 The Hindu god Ganesha, Lord of Success

14 A boy during his Sacred Thread ceremony

20 The decorated hands of a bride

How to use this book

Hinduism began in India, but there are now people all over the world who are **Hindus**. This book tells you what it is like to be Hindu and about the special times, customs and beliefs of Hindus.

Finding your way

The pages in this book have been carefully planned to make it easy for you to find out about Hinduism. Here are two examples with explanations about the different features. Look at the Contents pages too, to read about each section.

6 Birth

Celebrating a new life

The birth of a new baby is a special time for every family. It's the start of a new life, full of hope. Hindus believe it is one of 16 important events in a person's life, which they mark with a special ceremony called a **samskar**.

Before the birth

A little while before the birth, the family prepares to welcome the new baby. When the mother can feel the baby moving, the family has a special celebration. A **brahmin** (Hindu priest) comes to the celebration and prays to God to protect the baby.

There is another celebration just before the baby is expected. There is a big party at the **mandir** (temple) for family and friends. Everyone says prayers for the mother and brings a present for the baby.

A pregnant woman and her unborn baby are blessed during a ceremony called the Simanta samskar.

Bold words in the text are explained more fully in the glossary on page 30.

Captions give a short description of a picture.

Boxed text gives extra information about a subject on the page.

Comments give additional information about something specific in a picture.

Over to you... asks the reader to think more about their own customs and beliefs and how they compare to Hindu beliefs.

Samskars

A samskar is a Hindu ceremony that marks an important event in life. There are 16 samskars. Each one marks a person's entry into a different stage in life. These include:

● Jatakarma (4th samskar), performed just after the birth of a baby
● Upanayana (10th samskar), the Sacred Thread ceremony when a child begins school
● Antyeshti (16th samskar), a person's funeral, which is the last samskar.

Honey and ghee

The Jatakarma samskar takes place on the day a baby is born.

The birth ceremony

When a baby is born, honey and ghee (a kind of butter) are dabbed on the baby's tongue. Hindus believe that this will help the baby to grow up to be healthy and clever.

A close member of the family whispers the name of God in the baby's ear. This welcomes the baby into God's family and encourages the baby to live a good life.

Poonam is 8 years old. She lives in the UK. Her baby brother has just arrived.

Something wonderful happened today. I have a new baby brother! He doesn't have a name yet and his face is wrinkled like my grandpa Alok. When my mum found out she was going to have a baby, everyone was so happy. When the baby started to move inside her, we had a party at home. Dad wore white and Mum wore her white salwar kameez (traditional Asian outfit) with a red sash. A priest came to pray for my baby brother and everyone had a great time.

When a Hindu person dies

This painting depicts the idea of reincarnation. It shows someone in several different lives until they find God.

Hindus believe that a person is made up of two parts: a body and a soul. They believe that their soul is their spiritual part. Although their physical body will eventually die, their soul will go on living for ever.

Life after death

Hindus believe that after they die, their soul will be reborn into a new body on Earth. This is called **reincarnation**. They will continue to be reborn over and over again in this cycle. This is the Hindu cycle of life.

Moksha

After being reborn many times, the soul begins to tire, but the cycle ends only when a Hindu finds God. This is called **moksha**. It means breaking free from the feeling of having a body and being born again. Moksha is a state of discovering and merging with God. The **Bhagavad Gita** (Hindu sacred book) explains the soul's journey.

Pinda cake is made from three handfuls of boiled rice, fragrant flowers and leaves.

As a man casts off his worn-out clothes and takes on other new ones, so does the embodied soul cast off his worn-out bodies and enter other new ones ...
When we wear out clothes, we get new ones. When the body is worn out, the soul gets a new body.

Funeral of a loved one

The death of a loved one is a very sad time, but Hindus take comfort from the belief that their soul will continue. Krishna, an incarnation of God, said that death cannot be avoided.

In India, the body is wrapped in a cloth and cremated (burned) on a special fire called a funeral pyre. In the UK, the family has a funeral called a **cremation**. The family then takes the ashes to India to scatter on the holy River Ganga. Some families scatter the ashes on a river in their home country if they cannot get to India.

Pinda cakes are offered to the spirit of a dead person.

Over to you...

● Most religions teach that there is a life after death. What do you believe happens when people die?

Case studies give a Hindu person's own experience of a custom described in the section.

Quotes come from different Hindu teachings.

Celebrating a new life

The birth of a new baby is a special time for every family. It's the start of a new life, full of hope. Hindus believe it is one of 16 important events in a person's life, which they mark with a special ceremony called a **samskar**.

Before the birth

A little while before the birth, the family prepares to welcome the new baby. When the mother can feel the baby moving, the family has a special celebration. A **brahmin** (Hindu priest) comes to the celebration and prays to God to protect the baby.

There is another celebration just before the baby is expected. There is a big party at the **mandir** (temple) for family and friends. Everyone says prayers for the mother and brings a present for the baby.

A pregnant woman and her unborn baby are blessed during a ceremony called the Simanta samskar.

Samskars

A samskar is a Hindu ceremony that marks an important event in life. There are 16 samskars. Each one marks a person's entry into a different stage in life. These include:

- Jatakarma (4th samskar), performed just after the birth of a baby
- Upanayana (10th samskar), the Sacred Thread ceremony when a child begins school
- Antyeshti (16th samskar), a person's funeral, which is the last samskar.

Honey and ghee

The Jatakarma samskar takes place on the day a baby is born.

The birth ceremony

When a baby is born, honey and ghee (a kind of butter) are dabbed on the baby's tongue. Hindus believe that this will help the baby to grow up to be healthy and clever.

A close member of the family whispers the name of God in the baby's ear. This welcomes the baby into God's family and encourages the baby to live a good life.

Poonam is 8 years old. She lives in the UK. Her baby brother has just arrived.

Something wonderful happened today. I have a new baby brother! He doesn't have a name yet and his face is wrinkled like my grandpa Alok. When my mum found out she was going to have a baby, everyone was so happy. When the baby started to move inside her, we had a party at home. Dad wore white and Mum wore her white salwar kameez (traditional Asian outfit) with a red sash. A priest came to pray for my baby brother and everyone had a great time.

Choosing a name for a baby

Choosing the right name for a baby is very important. A priest helps parents to choose a name for for their baby to live up to. They choose a name to inspire the baby to live a good life.

*This baby has a black **tilak** (mark on her forehead). It is made from coal dust. This comes from a fire lit as a sacrifice to God.*

The right name

Parents hope that the name they choose will describe their baby's personality and identity. A baby boy might be given the name Satya. This means 'truthful'. The parents hope that this will encourage him to be truthful. A baby girl might be called Harsha, which means 'cheerful'.

A fire is lit to God during daily worship.

Over to you...

- How did your family celebrate when you were born?

- What does your name mean? Why was it chosen for you?

The naming ceremony

The Hindu naming ceremony is called Namakarana. It is a samskar. The whole family, including cousins, uncles, aunts and grandparents, goes to the mandir for the ceremony.

The baby has a tilak marked on her forehead with coloured paste. This symbolises the beginning of her spiritual life. The priest lays the baby on a bed of rice to show the hope that she will never go hungry. He whispers her name in her ear three times and says:

A father gives his baby honey and ghee on a gold ring during the Namakarana ceremony. This is to wish her good health and a long life.

"This is your name, which makes you who you are.
Welcome to the world."

Beginning a spiritual journey

Before children are three years old, Hindu families have a hair-cutting ceremony for them. This is the Mundan samskar. It is a sign that a child is starting a spiritual journey through life as a Hindu.

A new life as a Hindu

Before the Mundan ceremony, parents pray to the god Ganesha that their child will be healthy and happy. Ganesha is the lord of success, so Hindus pray to him when they start anything new.

Neepa is 9 years old. She has just been to her brother's Mundan samskar in London.

Cutting off a child's hair shows that the child is beginning a new life as a Hindu. A tuft of hair is left on the back of the head. This is called the shikha and is a symbol of protecting the child's memory.

Today was my brother Hemant's hair-cutting ceremony. One of Dad's friends shaved off Hemant's hair — all except for a tuft at the back to protect his memory. Then we sat around a small fire on the floor and prayed to the fire god Agni. The fire smelled really nice because we threw in ghee and grains for good luck. Afterwards we had a big meal with all our friends and family and they gave us presents.

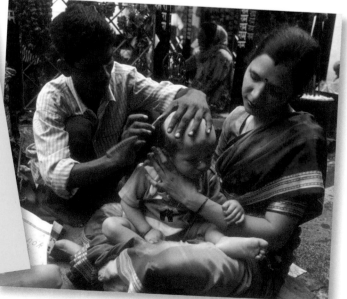

A child has his hair shaved.

Prayers around the fire

When the child's hair has been cut, the family sit around a fire. The fire at Hindu celebrations is called a **havan**. Prayers are given to the fire god Agni, the messenger who takes prayers to heaven. People chant **mantras** (prayers and hymns) too.

The havan is thought to bring health, wealth and happiness.

One God

Hindus believe that there is only one God, but they think about God in many different ways. These different forms of God look different and have different names. Think of it like ice and water, which are the same thing in different forms. Ganesha is a popular Hindu god. He is easy to recognise because he has the head of an elephant.

Starting school and growing up

Starting school is a special time for all children. Hindu boys and girls also start to learn about Hinduism and what their religion teaches them. Starting school and growing up is one of four main Stages of Life for Hindus.

Every child's special day

At about the age of five, Hindu children begin the first Stage of Life, called Brahmacharya. They go to school to learn. They must respect their teachers and elders and always try hard. Hindus believe that when children start school, they also start their spiritual education. Leaders at the mandir teach them how to behave properly and choose what is good and right over what is easy and enjoyable.

Ideas about respect for elders and what is right and wrong are often taught through stories from the **Ramayana** and **Mahabharata**. These are two ancient Indian poetry texts that are very important to Hindus. The story about Rama and Sita on page 16 of this book is from the Ramayana.

A woman reads the Ramayana with her grandchild.

Stages of Life

Hindus believe that there are four main Stages of Life:

- *Starting school and growing up (Brahmacharya)*
- *Getting married and starting a family (Grihastha)*
- *Getting older and then retiring (Vanaprastha)*
- *The final years of a Hindu's life, spent praying and* **meditating** *(Sannyasa)*

Over to you...

Who helps you to learn about and understand what is right and wrong? Make a list of people at school and at home who do this.

Ganesha is the Hindu god of education. He is also the lord of success and remover of obstacles.

Young Hindu boys learn about the god Ganesha from a comic book.

Neha is 5 years old. She lives in the UK. She has just started school.

At primary school I learn lots of different subjects, and my favourite is maths. At home, my mum and dad teach me about Hinduism. It is about behaving properly as well as believing in God. My dad told me to put some salt in a glass of water. "Where is the salt?" he said. I said I couldn't see the salt but I could taste it. "That's like God," said my dad. "You might not be able to see him, but he is everywhere in the world."

Sacred Thread ceremony

When a Hindu boy is ready to begin his education, he takes part in a Sacred Thread ceremony. This is the tenth samskar, called Upanayana. It is an exciting time for a Hindu boy.

A boy wears a yellow Sacred Thread (the thin cotton thread). It is actually three threads twisted three times and tied together.

Becoming responsible

Before the Sacred Thread ceremony, a boy's parents take him to the mandir to see the brahmin. At home, a havan is lit and prayers are chanted. Three cotton threads are laid over the boy's left shoulder. The three threads symbolise the respect that the boy should show to God, his parents and his **guru** (religious teacher).

The Sacred Thread shows that the boy is now a full member of the Hindu community. He is now allowed to study the **Vedas** (the Hindu sacred books) and help with the worship ceremony at home. The ceremony also marks that, from now on, the boy is old enough to be responsible for his actions.

*A priest leads the **puja** (worship) at a Sacred Thread ceremony. The adult men are wearing their own Sacred Threads across their shoulders.*

Ajay is 7 years old. He explains how he feels now he has taken part in the Upanayana.

I feel very grown up now and I know it is important to be a good Hindu in my community. My religion teaches me that I should try to do the right thing rather than just do the things that seem easy. Once, I was coming home from school and I saw my neighbour struggling with shopping bags. I wanted to get home to watch my favourite TV programme, but I stopped to help carry the bags.

Over to you...

● What special days and ceremonies are there for children in other religions?

● What are the similarities and differences between these ceremonies and the Upanayana?

The floor is decorated with rangoli (sand patterns) to spread joy and happiness.

A Hindu school in the UK

In the UK, many Hindu children go to ordinary schools, but some go to Hindu schools. At these schools, children are taught the same subjects as at an ordinary school but also have classes to learn about Hindu traditions and **culture**.

How are Hindu schools different?

Hindu schools are not that different from ordinary schools. Pupils are taught subjects such as maths and science, but they also learn about Hindu culture and traditions. Some schools teach Gujarati, a modern Indian language spoken in parts of India and other countries.

Hindu schools always provide a lunchtime meal that is alright for **vegetarians** because lots of Hindus don't eat meat. The food can be Western or Indian.

Prince Rama and his wife, Sita.

The story of Divali

*The story of **Divali** describes how Prince Rama and his brother defeated the demon Ravana and rescued Rama's wife, Sita. They all returned to their kingdom after 14 years living in the forest. It was dark when they arrived home, so the people lit lamps along the streets so that they could find their way. The lights were called diva, which is where the name Divali comes from. The story teaches that good can win over evil and light can win over darkness.*

Anisha is 9 years old. She goes to a Hindu school in London.

At my school we learn about all subjects, just like at other schools, but we also learn other things. In performing arts we do singing and drama, but we also do bharat natyam, which is one of the oldest dance forms in India — a bit like folk dancing. I love learning about my culture and traditions and think it's very important. Our teachers say, "The heart of education is the education of the heart."

The movements of every part of the body help to tell the story.

Celebrating Divali

Hindu schools celebrate Hindu festivals. Divali is the most popular Hindu festival and is usually in October. It is the Hindu New Year, so school children get a day off school to celebrate. During the celebrations, children learn about their 'inner light' that outshines all darkness and bad things. It is a time to forgive and forget.

Hindu girls perform Divali dances. They tell stories of the Hindu gods.

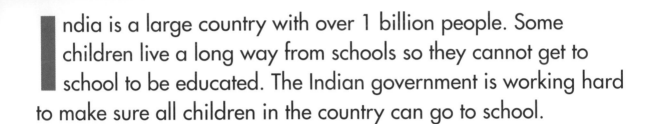

A Hindu school in India

I ndia is a large country with over 1 billion people. Some children live a long way from schools so they cannot get to school to be educated. The Indian government is working hard to make sure all children in the country can go to school.

Two sisters walk together to school in India.

Important stage of life

Education is very important in Hinduism. Hindus believe that people are born physically as babies, but spiritually when they begin their education. Children start primary school in India when they are 6 years old. They go to school until they are at least 14 years old, but many stay in full-time education until they are 17. Secondary school (11 to 15 years) is followed by higher secondary (16 to 17 years) and then it's off to university or college.

Learning languages

About 80 percent of people in India are Hindus, and there are also Muslims, Christians and Sikhs. Hindi is the most widely spoken language, but there are 21 other official languages! The language children learn at school depends on where they live, although many learn Hindi and English as well as their own language.

Leaving school

At the end of the Brahmacharya (student) Stage of Life, Hindus are ready to get married. They have grown up and are ready to take on adult responsibilities. This is why finishing education is so important to Hindus.

Mahendra is 8 years old.
He lives in Kolkata, India.

I go to a Hindu school in Kolkata. It's for boys aged 6 to 19. The primary classes are from 7am until 9.30am. After school I do my homework and play football with my friends. Sometimes I help my uncle in his shop. Before lessons, we say a prayer and sing India's national anthem. At primary school we study Bengali, English, maths, science, social studies, environment, creative arts, history, geography, technology and media. When I get to secondary school, I can specialise in science, arts, business or humanities. If I choose arts, I can study **Sanskrit**, an ancient, sacred language of Hindus, but Mum wants me to be an engineer or a doctor.

Some children practise puja at their school in India.

A havan is lit by a teacher, who leads the worship.

The meaning of marriage

Getting married and starting a family is the beginning of Grihastha, the second Stage of Life. A Hindu wedding is a bond between two people and also between two families. It's an exciting and happy day for everyone involved.

Seema lives in the UK. She is about to get married.

Tomorrow I'm getting married. I'm so happy! Our wedding ceremony is planned on a very lucky day. My friends are coming over for a party tonight. We'll have our hands and feet decorated with paint made from the henna plant and there will be lots of laughing and joking — and eating! Because our wedding is in the UK, we're having a civil ceremony in a register office in the morning. Then we'll all get ready for the big, colourful, noisy, traditional Hindu wedding at the temple.

A bond between two souls

Hindus believe that marriage is a sacred duty and something God expects them to do. They also believe that the bond of marriage can continue even beyond death.

Hindu weddings involve many **rituals**. They are different in different parts of the world, but there are some important things that stay the same in all Hindu traditions.

● Marriage is the joining of two **souls** in a sacred bond of love and commitment. (The soul is the spiritual part of a person.)
● There are blessings from the couple's parents, teachers and God.
● There is a big, joyful celebration with the couple's family and friends.

Water and fresh flowers are symbols of cleanliness and beauty.

The bride's hands and feet are decorated with red henna paint for success.

Symbols at the wedding

A Hindu wedding area is filled with lots of symbols. They all have different meanings and are very important to the bride and groom and their families. They show what their hopes are for the future marriage.

- Water washes away impurities.
- Coconut represents good luck and God.
- Fresh flowers (or flower petals) symbolise beauty.
- Rice symbolises wealth and children.
- Ghee butter is an offering to higher beings.
- Fire represents the fire god Agni – the witness to the wedding ceremony.

Hindus believe that coconut is the fruit of God. Using it in a ceremony is a symbol of God being there.

Traditional Hindu wedding

Hindu weddings are traditionally joyful and colourful. In the UK, most weddings happen in only one day, but in India a wedding might last for as long as five days! The wedding ceremony is called Vivah and is a holy samskar.

Wedding traditions

In Hinduism, different colours have special meanings. The bride wears a traditional red and gold wedding sari (a long dress made from one piece of cloth). Red is a symbol of good luck. Gold is a symbol of wealth. The groom often wears gold and white. White is a symbol of purity, wealth and wisdom.

The whole community is part of the celebration because of the importance Hindus place on being part of the community. In India, the groom's family dances from their home to the wedding. The groom may arrive in a large car, on horseback or on an elephant.

Musicians in traditional, colourful outfits play for a wedding dance in India.

Ghee and grains are offered to the fire to build a relationship with higher beings to gain health, wealth and happiness.

Wedding ceremony

The bride and groom get married in front of a havan under a **mandap** (a special canopy with four pillars). Then the couple walk around the fire four times. They also take seven steps together, called saptapadi. The steps represent health, wealth, strength, children, happiness, life-long friendship and God.

During the ceremony, the groom takes hold of the bride's hand and makes this marriage vow:

" I take hold of your hand so that together we may lead a long and happy life. "

A bride and groom sit under a mandap with friends during a wedding in India.

Over to you...

● What similarities can you see between Hindu weddings and any other weddings that you have been to?

Becoming a grown-up

Marriage is the start of Grihastha, the second Stage of Life. It's the longest Stage of Life and an important one. When Hindus get married, they become householders and must take care of children, older people, guests and the community.

Taking on responsibility

Grihastha starts when a person finishes their studies and is ready to start a family. It lasts until retirement. At this Stage of Life, Hindus take on the responsibility of earning money for their family. Men and women have different roles in the family, but they are all responsible for following the traditions of the Hindu religion. This is important because parents are the first teachers of children.

Amrish is 22. He trained as an engineer at university and now designs bridges and roads.

I think it's a great honour to earn money for my family, but it's a big responsibility, too. I must look after my family and pass on our traditions and beliefs to my children. Parents should teach their children Hindu values by setting a good example. I want all my children to work hard and get a good education. It's my job as a parent to help them to achieve this.

Over to you...

● Who teaches you about values? Make a list of the people who do this.

● Do people in your family have any different roles? What roles do they share?

A householder's prayer

Hindu women who are having children say this prayer to Agni, the fire god, asking him to help them to be a good householder.

A Hindu family gather for a photograph outisde a temple in London.

> *May I be a good Grihastha (householder), providing love, affection, devotion, courtesy and hospitality to everyone. Bless us with a long life.*

The family can include several generations.

Changing as we grow older

Vanaprastha is the third Stage of Life. It's a time when Hindus start thinking about more important things than objects and possessions. It begins when a householder stops being responsible for the family and the next generation takes over.

A husband and wife are blessed by their family on their 50th wedding anniversary.

Time to think

In the past, at the start of Vanaprastha, a person would retire from work to live a simpler life and spend more time thinking about God. Today, it's like retiring from the job of being a householder. Older men and women are respected as advisors.

Final Stage of Life

Sannyasa is the final Stage of Life for Hindus. At this stage, Hindus pray, meditate and think about God. They may do charitable things that will help their **karma** (the good and bad consequences of their actions).

Sannyasa can start at any age. It happens when a person feels strongly that they would like to live a religious life.

Over to you...

● Why do we feel bad if we do something bad? Why do we feel good if we do something good?

● Has anyone ever surprised you by doing something nice for you that you were not expecting?

What is karma?

Hindus believe that everything they do has consequences. If they act responsibly and do good things, their actions will have good results. If they don't act responsibly and do bad things, it will lead to difficulties. This is called karma. Our actions and the way we behave affects our karma in this life and the next.

Mahamati is 82 years old. He has five children, nine grandchildren and one great grandchild.

I love spending time with my grandchildren and Ajay, my great grandchild. I taught my children about karma and now I teach the young ones. I tell them that actions have consequences. Everything we do, think and say has an effect on us and others. I believe that if I treat people with kindness and respect, this is good and will bring good karma for my next life.

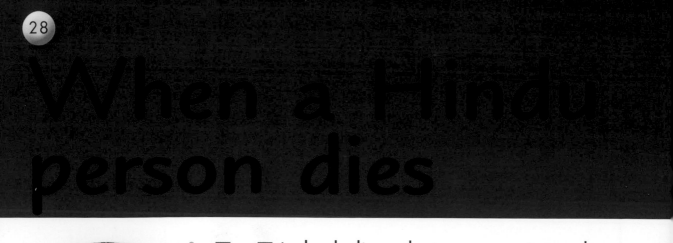

When a Hindu person dies

This painting depicts the idea of reincarnation. It shows someone in several different lives until they find God.

Hindus believe that a person is made up of two parts: a body and a soul. They believe that their soul is their spiritual part. Although their physical body will eventually die, their soul will go on living for ever.

Life after death

Hindus believe that after they die, their soul will be reborn into a new body on Earth. This is called **reincarnation**. They will continue to be reborn over and over again in this cycle. This is the Hindu cycle of life.

Moksha

After being reborn many times, the soul begins to tire, but the cycle ends only when a Hindu finds God. This is called **moksha**. It means breaking free from the feeling of having a body and being born again. Moksha is a state of discovering and merging with God. The **Bhagavad Gita** (Hindu sacred book) explains the soul's journey.

As a man casts off his worn-out clothes and takes on other new ones, so does the embodied soul cast off his worn-out bodies and enter other new ones ...

When we wear out clothes, we get new ones. When the body is worn out, the soul gets a new body.

> *Death happens to everyone who is born,*
> *and everyone who dies will be reborn.*
> *This can't be changed so there's no need to be sad.*

Pinda cake is made from three handfuls of boiled rice, fragrant flowers and leaves.

Over to you...

● Most religions teach that there is a life after death. What do you believe happens when people die?

Funeral of a loved one

The death of a loved one is a very sad time, but Hindus take comfort from the belief that their soul will continue. Krishna, an incarnation of God, said that death cannot be avoided.

In India, the body is wrapped in a cloth and cremated (burned) on a special fire called a funeral pyre. In the UK, the family has a funeral called a **cremation**. The family then takes the ashes to India to scatter on the holy River Ganga. Some families scatter the ashes on a river in their home country if they cannot get to India.

Pinda cakes are offered to the spirit of a dead person.

Glossary and more information

Bhagavad Gita (The Song of the Lord) A Hindu sacred book; part of the *Mahabharata*.

brahmin A term meaning 'One who is honest and peaceful', usually reserved for addressing a priest.

cremation A sort of funeral in which a body is burnt until it turns to ashes.

culture The art, customs and ideas of a particular group of people.

Divali The Festival of Lights, celebrated by many Hindus to mark the arrival of New Year.

guru A spiritual teacher.

havan A fire that is made during important ceremonies, to worship God.

Hindu One who believes there is one God called Brahman who created everything. Brahman takes on many different forms that some Hindus worship as gods or goddesses.

karma The good, or not so good, effect of our actions.

Mahabharata A long poem from ancient India that is very important to *Hindus*. It tells the story of a war between two branches of a family.

mandap A cloth roof supported on pillars, under which a bride and groom get married in a *Hindu* wedding ceremony.

mandir A place where *Hindus* worship.

mantra Prayers or hymns that *Hindus* chant to help them to concentrate on God.

meditating Concentrating very deeply.

moksha When the *soul* is set free from the cycle of life, death and rebirth.

puja Worship of God through, for example, prayers, offerings and *rituals*.

Ramayana A long poem from ancient India that is very important to *Hindus*. It tells a story of good overcoming evil.

reincarnation The rebirth of the *soul* into a new body on Earth.

ritual A religious ceremony in which a series of actions are performed in a set order.

samskar One of the 16 ceremonies or rites that a person goes through during their life.

Sanskrit An ancient language of India. Many *Hindu* sacred books are written in Sanskrit.

soul The spiritual part of a person, separate from the body.

tilak A mark put on the forehead to show that someone is a good *Hindu*.

Vedas The four ancient, sacred books that guide *Hindus* in their daily life.

vegetarian Someone who does not eat meat, fish or eggs.

Things to do

Ask your teacher to help you to organise a visit to your nearest mandir. The National Council of Hindu Temples has a list of temples in the UK. You can find out where your nearest temple is on the website www.nchtuk.org.

Before you go to a mandir, make a list of what you would like to find out about, for example:

● the building and the way that it's decorated
● the people who worship there
● the times when people go to pray or to celebrate
● the people who work there
● how you should behave when you visit a mandir

Read the exciting story of Rama and Sita and find out how they escaped from the demon Ravana, with the help of Hanuman, the monkey-god.

Ask your teacher if your class can celebrate Divali, the Hindu Festival of Lights. Visit the website www.diwalifestival.org to get some ideas on how to celebrate.

In Hinduism, colours have special meanings. Find out why red, yellow, green, saffron, white and blue are the most important colours to Hindus.

More information

Find out more about Hinduism from these websites.

Websites

www.hinduism.fsnet.co.uk
The Hinduism for Schools website is packed with information on Hinduism. There is a huge glossary, and you can hear all the words spoken in Sanksrit.

www.hindukids.org
This fun website is for younger children but still has lots of great information on Hinduism. It has pages on festivals, stories, prayers and also some games and a quiz.

www.holifestival.org
This is a great place to look if you want to find out about the Hindu festival of Holi. The colourful site includes information about legends to do with the festival, the colours of Holi and even recipes.

www.hinducounciluk.org
There is lots of information about Hinduism on this site and also a kids' corner, which explains Hinduism for younger children.

www.hinduacademy.org
The Hindu Academy is dedicated to educating people about Hinduism. Its website gives lots of information about the organisation and a useful list of dates and places where talks and classes on Hinduism are held.

Index

Picture credits

The publisher would like to thank the following for their kind permission to reproduce their photographs:

Position key: c=centre; b=bottom; t=top; l=left; r=right

1c: L B Duran/World Religions Photo Library; 3br: Dallas Events Inc/shutterstock; 6bl: C Boulanger/World Religions Photo Library; 7bc: Tracy Whiteside/shutterstock; 7cr: Danny Smythe/shutterstock; 7tr: Linda & Colin McKie/istockphoto; 7tl: Glenda Powers;

8bc: L B Duran/World Religions Photo Library; 9c: L B Duran/World Religions Photo Library; 10br: Nick Dawson/World Religions Photo Library; 10bl: vivek/shutterstock; 11tc: Chinch Gryniewicz/World Religions Photo Library; 12bl: Christine Osbourne/World Religions Photo Library; 13tc: Nick Dawson/World Religions Photo Library; 13bl: Tracy Whiteside/shutterstock; 15bc: L B Duran/World Religions Photo Library; 15tl: Rohit Seth/shutterstock; 17c: A Masi/World Religions Photo Library; 17tl: Tracy Whiteside/shutterstock; 18cl: Loic Bernard/iStockphoto; 19bc: G B Mukherji/World Religions Photo Library; 19tl: Arvind Balaraman/shutterstock; 20cl: Jason

Stitt/shutterstock; 20br: Liv friis-larsen/shutterstock; 21br: fotosav/shutterstock; 21br: Subbotina Anna/shutterstock; 21tc: Dallas Events Inc/shutterstock; 22bc: Prem Kapoor/World Religions Photo Library; 23tc: Prem Kapoor/World Religions Photo Library; 24bc: William Holtby/CIRCA Religions Photo Library; 24cl: Kharidehal Abhirama Ashwin/shutterstock; 26bc: Chinch Gryniewicz/World Religions Photo Library; 27tc: A Masi/World Religions Photo Library; 27bl: Arvind Balaraman/shutterstock; 29cl: L B Duran/World Religions Photo Library

Cover photograph © Corbis Premium RF/Alamy